ANCIENT CIVILIZATIONS

THE
PERSIANS
WARRIORS OF THE ANCIENT WORLD

by
KATHERINE REECE

Rourke
Publishing LLC
Vero Beach, Florida 32964

www.rourkepublishing.com

PHOTO CREDITS:
Courtesy Ashmolean Museum: page 21; Courtesy Charles Reasoner: pages 17, 34; Courtesy www.freestockphotos.com: pages 15, 18, 26, 36; Courtesy Khodadad Rezakhani, www.iranologie.com: page 40; Courtesy Kiarash Yashayai, www.photospreview.com: cover, title, pages 7, 8, 10, 19, 27, 29; Courtesy NASA: page 6; Courtesy Rohm Padilla: pages 25, 38, 44; Courtesy Wildsmith Gallery: pages 9, 32

DESIGN AND LAYOUT: ROHM PADILLA

Library of Congress Cataloging-in-Publication Data

Reece, Katherine E., 1955-
    The Persians : warriors of the ancient world / Katherine Reece.
        p. cm. -- (Ancient civilizations)
    Includes bibliographical references and index.
    ISBN 1-59515-238-5 (hardcover)
    1. Iran--Civilization--To 640--Juvenile literature.   I. Title.   II.
Series: Reece, Katherine E., 1955-   Ancient civilizations.
    DS267.R44 2004
    935--dc22

                    2004012112

TITLE PAGE IMAGE
Detail of Persian soldiers from the palace at Persepolis

TABLE OF CONTENTS

INTRODUCTION

Every day we use money to pay for things, but who first made and used coins to buy what they needed? If you walk through a pretty garden in the springtime, do you ever wonder when flowers and shrubs may have first been planted for the sheer pleasure of enjoying their beauty? Do you take roads and freeways for granted? Who first built a system of roads for speedy transport? What was the model for the many styles of governments we have today?

Early Elamite nomads loading a camel

For answers to these questions, we look to one of the greatest **empires** of the ancient world, which evolved during the 6th century in present-day **Iran**. Iran actually means "land of Aryan," which was the name given to the people called Aryans who moved into the area. These **nomads** who came from western Asia were later called **Persis** by the Greeks, and the vast empire they built and ruled became known as **Persia**.

Diversity and tolerance were characteristics of the Persian culture. Persians were open to influence from abroad and took up the languages and ideas of those they conquered. The Persians united very different people–Indians, **Medes**, Babylonians, **Lydians**, Greeks, Jews, **Phoenicians**, and Egyptians–all under one empire in such a way that secured peace and prosperity for each region.

People from all over the world still make journeys to holy sites in Iran, such as this tomb of a religious leader.

CHAPTER 1:
WHERE WAS ANCIENT PERSIA?

As early as 5000 **B.C.E.**, settlers began living on the high plateaus of Aryan. Located between the **steppes** of Asia and the **Fertile Crescent** were two deserts, which were rimmed by fertile plateaus. To the north were high mountains leading into Asia. The lower ranges of mountains bordered present-day Afghanistan and Pakistan. On the western side loomed the Zagros Mountains and to the north were the rugged Elburz Mountains. The land consisted of dry basins of salt and sand, some marshlands, high volcanic mountain chains, and narrow coastal plains.

ARABIAN SEA

SAUDI ARABIAN PENINSULA

GULF OF OMAN

STRAIT OF HORMUZ

ZAGROS MOUNTAINS

SALT DESERT

This photograph looks southwest across modern Iran, toward the Strait of Hormuz and tip of the Saudi Arabian Peninsula. The terrain is a rugged, arid landscape of dry salt basins and mountain ranges. The lakes in the lower left corner are normally dry lake beds in the southwest corner of Afghanistan.

At the edge of the salt deserts at the base of the mountains were many rich fertile plains that grew with water flowing from the mountains. These areas served well for feeding livestock and growing crops.

The climate was a combination of long, hot summers and cold, rainy winters with the mountainous regions of the north and west being subtropical. Temperatures and rainfall or snowfall varied with mountainous elevations, as winds brought moisture from the Persian Gulf. The Caspian region might receive more than 40 inches (102 cm) of rain each year. Average annual rainfall was only about 5 inches (12.7 cm) along the coastal plains and central portion of the plateau, with temperatures reaching as high as 120° F (49° C).

Despite the harsh landscape, the early settlers harnessed the water from the rivers and snow that ran off the mountains in the spring. Persians began to build canals and ditches to bring precious water to their fields. In these fertile areas, nomads found a perfect place for growing crops such as wheat and barley. They soon **domesticated** wild animals such as cattle and sheep and began to settle in communities.

The rugged Elburz Mountains located in the north of Persia run along the southern edge of the Caspian Sea.

This region eventually became the bridge between the developing eastern and western civilizations of Mesopotamia and Egypt. The rich plateaus attracted waves of nomadic tribes. During 1000 B.C.E., two Aryan tribes moved from the north and settled in the area. The Medes made their homes in the Zagros Mountains, with their rich mineral deposits of gold, silver, and semiprecious stones. In ancient times, this area became known as Lydia. The Medes are remembered in history for creating the first coins to be used in trade. The second tribe moved near the edge of the Tigris River valley in an old kingdom called **Elam** and **Pars**, to form the Persia of ancient times.

CHAPTER III

CYRUS THE GREAT

Cyrus the Great

Wars in ancient times started over the need for more water and control of land. Not only did possession of additional land provide natural borders for protection, but men from the region were recruited for armies. Conquering lands was nothing new during this period, but the methods of conquest used by the Persians were quite different. The Persian rulers of the Achaemenid Dynasty never shamed or hurt the pride of the people they conquered. Rather than using brute force, they successfully negotiated with the people and provided for the needs of the conquered territory in order to gain the cooperation and loyalty of each new addition to their empire.

Cyrus II, also known as Cyrus the Great, was born in 598 B.C.E and lived until 529 B.C.E. He was the first king of a united Persia and was responsible for building the largest empire of the world at that time. He came to power in 549 B.C.E. and began his rule by conquering his neighbors, the Medes. This conquest gave him access to the rich mineral reserves of gold and silver buried in the Zagros Mountains. The Medes, as well as each new region that was added to the Persian Empire, paid tribute to the King of Persia.

A statue called the Guardian Angel, from the palace of Cyrus

CHAPTER IV

DARIUS I

King Darius enthroned sits beneath the Ahura Mazda symbol on the doorway of the Council Hall at Persepolis in Iran.

Darius I expanded his kingdom into the Indus Valley and westward to **Macedonia**. By this time, the Persian Empire covered more than 2 million square miles (5,179,976 sq km) and contained more than 10 million people. Whereas the kings before Darius I had devoted their energy to conquering lands to build the vast Persian Empire, Darius spent his time building a sound system for government.

Darius I secured his rule by gaining the cooperation of local rulers, but he also divided his empire into 20 provinces, or **satrapies**. Each satrapie was under the rule of a **satrap**, or local governor, who was appointed by Darius I.

This illustration of Darius I is made from the largest cuneiform inscription of all. It is carved 340 feet (104 m) above the ground in the face of a cliff in Behistun, Iran. The inscription contains more than 1,300 lines of text written in three languages, and provided the key that allowed archaeologists to decipher cuneiform writing.

The satrap was usually a prince from the Persian royal family or a nobleman of the elite class of Persians.

Satraps were usually princes or members of royal families. Above is a relief showing a Persian nobleman locked in battle with a horned creature.

Large numbers of soldiers enlisted in the Persian army from many of the provinces that were conquered. These soldiers held a high place in Persian society and were even relied upon to supply the king with information about his royal subjects.

The satrap was responsible for all government functions within his province. He collected all taxes and tributes to be paid to the king. He would oversee economic development of trade and agriculture. Justice for the people of his province was his responsibility. Satraps were given the freedom to make all decisions necessary for their province, but they still answered directly to the king. Within each province, the

Relief of a high-ranking Persian soldier taken from Persepolis

individual regions and cities were ruled by local people of the conquered land.

To prevent the abuse of power, Darius I also had Royal Inspectors who oversaw the satraps. These officials were called the "King's Eyes and Ears" and reported directly to the king. From the many lands and regions, large numbers of soldiers were enlisted for the Persian army. These professional soldiers not only protected the borders of the provinces, but since they answered only to the king, they also kept the satraps from becoming too powerful.

ROYAL SECRETARIES

Royalty relied upon their scribes to write and read correspondence for the realm. Records show that the kings themselves often could neither read nor write.

With such a vast empire and so many languages among the different provinces, Darius I knew the only way to rule his subjects was to use one common language. Therefore, **Old Persian** became the official language for the empire. Instead of the **cuneiform** writing of Mesopotamia, Darius borrowed the Phoenician alphabet for all his recordkeeping.

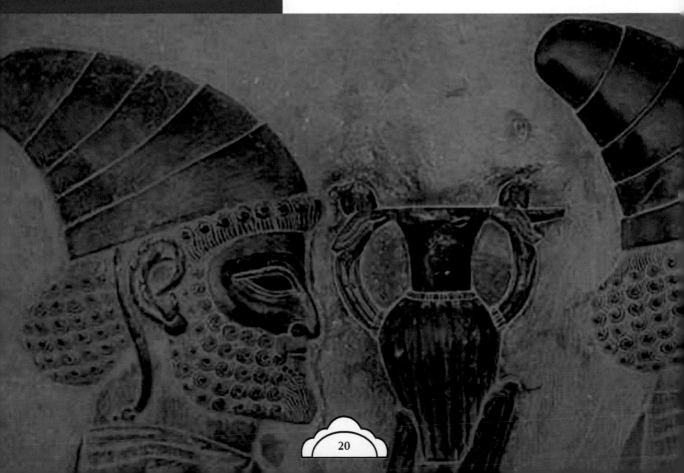

Darius I created an army of scribes to keep track of the many tributes collected from all his conquered lands. Provinces paid the tribute with their homeland resources. If the region was agricultural, the king collected one-fifth of the harvest. Other provinces might send sheep, horses, mules, minerals, or precious stones. Babylon was taxed 500 boys each year to be servants in the royal palace. Taxes were a small price to pay for the benefits of peace and protection provided by the king. One common language and the removal of barriers between provinces unified Persia, while at the same time making its citizens wealthy.

ARCHERS

Persians borrowed the concept of coinage for trade and taxes from the Lydians whom they conquered. A standard coin in the Persian empire was the **daric**, which was about the size of a dime and was made of pure gold. On one side was the image of the king holding a bow, so it got the nickname of an "archer."

Many Persian nobles came from other societies, such as these Syrians shown here paying tribute to the king.

A Persian and a
Greek soldier fighting

Tributes flowed into the royal Persian treasury and the taxes paid for palaces, roads, and canals. Darius I began building a ceremonial city to honor the Persian kings of the Achaemenian empire. Work began in 509 B.C.E at Persepolis in the Pars province and continued with successive kings, who each added their own palaces to the grounds. Persepolis was located in the homeland of the Achaemenids and became its spiritual center. It was also the site of the royal treasury, and each spring the kings came to celebrate the festival of the New Year. The beautiful capital stood until it was burned in 331 B.C.E. by a 23-year-old Greek warrior by the name of **Alexander the Great**. Yet the great empire and capital had survived for 150 years after the death of Darius I.

Darius I also rebuilt the old Elamite capital of Susa using materials and labor from distant provinces. He brought cedars from Lebanon and timber from **Carmania** in southern Persia and **Gandhara**, now known as Afghanistan. Gold came from **Sardis** in Lydia and Bactria, 1,000 miles (1,609 km) away beside the Oxus River in the foothills of the Hindu Kush, or present-day Uzbekistan. Ivory came from Egypt and Ethiopia in Africa and Sind on the threshold of India. Stonecutters from Ionia, goldsmiths from Media, brick masons from Babylon, and wood workers from Egypt combined their skills to make Susa one of the most beautiful cities in the Persian Empire.

Garden in modern Iran

A GARDEN PARADISE

From the Persians, we have the word, "paradise." Their **paradesios**-or enclosures-were walled gardens or parks created for the king's pleasure. Since Persians lived in such an arid country, they created well-watered green spaces filled with trees, shrubs, and flowers. To keep the plants green and sweet, they were planted in neat rows between stone **conduits** that carried water.

THE ROYAL ROAD

Built by Darius I to connect outlying provinces to the Persian capital of Persepolis, this road connected 111 stations and was 1,600 miles (2,575 km) long. Cyrus the Great built a series of posting stations to his provinces one day's ride apart. At the stations were relays of horses and a man in charge who handled messages. If a message was urgent, the relay would go through the night.

Tributes also paid for roads that connected the satrapies to the center of the Persian Empire at Persepolis. With new roads, messengers on horseback traveling 200 miles (322 km) per day could quickly inform the king of any developing problems throughout his far-reaching empire. With these roads protected by the king's armies, travel was safe for all Persian citizens.

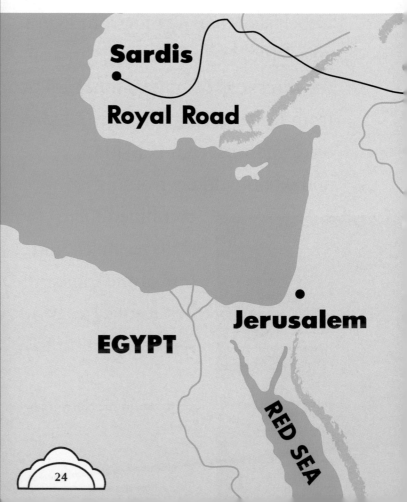

Sardis

Royal Road

Jerusalem

EGYPT

RED SEA

CHAPTER V:
TRADE BY LAND AND SEA

The vast expanse of the Persian Empire provided for a large variety of raw minerals, agricultural products, craftsmen's skills, and knowledge to move freely among its many provinces. The trade routes were well-protected highways, and control of the Mediterranean Sea allowed Persia to trade with more distant lands. Darius I even built a canal from the Nile River to the Gulf of Suez so that his ships could travel more easily from Egypt to Persia. All the countries in the Persian Empire prospered by the exchange of goods. Whatever was lacking in one province was supplied by another.

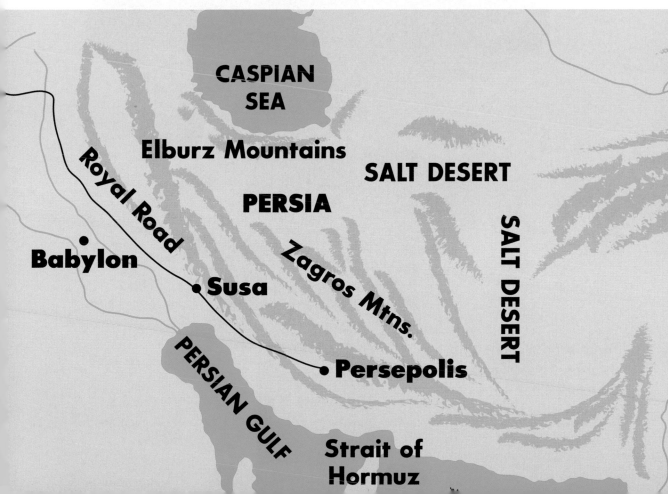

CHAPTER VI:
PERSIAN ART AND ARCHITECTURE

The mingling of different people and ideas created new expressions in art. The Persians were eager to combine new forms of art with their own, and a beautiful and colorful civilization was the result. The capital of Persepolis is a rich example of the how the diversity of cultures within the empire created new forms of artistic expression.

These solid marble bulls decorate this column that supported part of the roof of a building.

The site of Persepolis is a rocky point jutting out from a line of low hills. It faces west and overlooks a broad, fertile plain. The point was cut down to create a level platform. From the plain below, a great staircase led up to the platform and ended at an entrance gate. Just inside the gate was the **portico** of "all lands," which was guarded by huge human-headed, winged bulls carved out of stone brought from **Nineveh**.

(Above) one of the winged, human-headed bulls that guards the portico of "all lands" at Persepolis. (Below) a view of the staircase of the Palace of Darius

THE APADANA

A great audience hall was the central feature of the capitals of Persepolis and Susa. The apadana in Susa had 36 columns that could be seen from the distance.

To the south of the portico stood the great apadana, or audience hall. The walls of the apadana and its double staircase were built of stone decorated with carved images of Persian guards in their distinctive Persian and Median dress and long lines of subjects of the empire bringing their offerings for the New Year festival. The hall had six rows of six massive columns, which held up a flat roof covering the entire structure.

Carved figures decorate the central stairway of the Apadana in Persepolis.

To the east of the apadana was yet another hall made up of 100 stone columns. Assyrian columns covered with Egyptian designs rose 60 feet (18.3 m) and supported a structure that measured 40,000 square feet (3,716 sq meters).

The art of the Persians was greatly influenced by neighboring civilizations. This column in the shape of a giant bird at Persepolis looks like many examples from Egypt.

(Above) a giant stone column with the top carved in the shape of a bull. (Below) a detail of the same carving.

Designs, elements, and details from buildings seen in distant lands were used in creating the beauty of Persepolis. From Assyria came the idea of a royal structure being placed on a raised platform, the use of colossal stone bulls, and the composition and style of incised stonework. The influence of Egyptian art brought decorative elements and profiles used in making ornate moldings.

Persepolis was backed by a bare mountainside into which the tomb of Darius I was cut into the face of the cliffs. By contrast, the tomb of Cyrus the Great was built out on the open **Murghab** plain. By stacking large blocks of stone almost 35 feet (10.7 m) high, the tomb of Cyrus the Great took on the look of a Mesopotamian ziggurat combined with the features of an Anatolian tomb. Carved on the tomb are these words, "I am Cyrus, who founded the empire of the Persians. Grudge me not therefore, this little earth that covers my body."

The Tomb of Darius I is carved into the cliff that acts as a backdrop to the Persepolis site.

(Above) a necklace made from ancient carnelian beads. (Below) amethyst was only one of the many types of stones Persians used in making jewelry.

Persia became known for its polished gray pottery, as well as its skill in creating beautiful jewelry. Thick carpets with intricately woven designs unique to the different people of the empire were in high demand. Gold and silver bracelets, earrings, pendants, and necklaces were bought and sold. Beads of gold, carnelian, coral, amethyst, and lapis lazuli were fashioned into colorful and expensive ornaments. Designs in jewelry would often take on the forms of animals, bells, flowers, or geometric shapes. From Egypt, Persian artisans learned the skill of inlaying precious stones to create beautiful jewelry.

This necklace is made from ancient beads of lapis lazuli, glass, and gold.

CHAPTER VII:
WHAT DID THE PERSIANS WEAR?

Persians preferred to mix colorful floral designs with solid or striped fabrics in their clothing. Fashions made of cotton, wool, linen, and silk dyed in earth tones soon gave way to vibrantly colored material brought in from faraway markets. Both women and men wore loose drawstring pants called sherwals. For the wealthy, the sherwal was made looser and wider in design. Women's sherwals were tapered at the ankle.

Over their sherwals, women would wear draped gowns with a colorful **sash** tied at the hip. Men wore tunics to their knees with a sash tied around the waist. These sashes provided a place to carry a knife or moneybag. Tunics could vary in length, with sleeves that were wide, narrow, or long, but they all shared a common feature–the Persians' love of bright colors.

Persian nobles dressed in rich, colorful robes

(Left) a Persian soldier with a sword and staff. (Right) a Persian nobleman with a sword and scepter

(Below) a Persian woman enjoys flowers in her garden. Her head is covered in a traditional cloth, which has been the custom since ancient times.

Royalty draped themselves with gold necklaces strung with carnelians, emeralds, jasper, and amethyst. Their earrings were studded with turquoise and lapis lazuli. Common people could not have afforded precious metals and stones, but craftsmen provided intricate designs in jewelry for them as well.

The clothing of this (left) Mede nobleman, and (center) Persian nobleman is very decorative compared to the Persian on the right.

CHAPTER VIII:
WHAT DID THE PERSIANS EAT?

With crops grown throughout its empire, Persians enjoyed a rich diet. The most common grains of rice, barley, and wheat could be combined with vegetables, dates, oranges, and lemons mixed with spices to make dishes that were both colorful and flavorful. Grains were ground to make flour and bake various types of bread. Meat came from Persia's vast herds of cattle, sheep, and goats.

Meat from wild and domesticated mountain goats was used for food.

Orange trees grew well in the arid climate and provided a sweet fruit snack.

Dates on a palm branch

Wild game was hunted for sport as well as for food. Kings and noblemen would organize hunts to kill any animals that preyed on livestock. Citizens would gather on nearby hillsides to witness the skill of the king as he risked his life to defend his people against dangerous lions.

A lion is shown here attacking a bull on a relief from the facade of the stairway of the Apadana at Persepolis.

CHAPTER IX:

RELIGION IN PERSIA

Religion in Persia embodied the beliefs and customs of all those regions that had been conquered. By the time the rule of Darius I ended, **Zoroastrianism** was the religion practiced by most Persians. Central beliefs were rooted in sacrifice and the element of fire and were based on the teachings of the prophet, Zoroaster.

A major symbol of Zoroastrianism and ancient Persia is the Ahura Mazda. By the time of the Achaemenid dynasty it had already been in use in various forms around the Middle East and Egypt.

Zoroaster claimed he had a divine revelation that revealed that there was a god of justice, kindness, and generosity, not vengeance. Two gods, equal in power, had created for mankind a constant struggle between good and evil, darkness and light. **Ahura Mazda**, or the Wise One, was the god of goodness and light, and behavior guided by a moral code gained his favor. Ahura Mazda was opposed by Ahriman, meaning "Destructive Spirit," who was associated with wickedness and death. The battle between good and evil was believed to someday lead to the destruction of all evil. Zoroastrianism united the Persian people with a belief in one god instead of many.

FIRE AND "ASHA"

As a symbol of "Asha" and the "original light of God," fire holds a special place of esteem in Zoroastrianism. Prayer is often done in front of a fire, and fires dedicated to their god burn at all times without interruption in the major temples. Asha is a key concept in the religion and relates to truth, righteousness, world order, eternal law, and fitness.

Zoroastrianism taught that those who led lives of good deeds would be rewarded with life after death. At the time of death, final judgment determined if a soul would have everlasting life or be sentenced to hell. Hell was described as a temporary place of suffering for those who had not done good deeds while waiting for the day when Ahriman would finally be defeated. At that time the souls in hell would be released to join all others with Ahura Mazda.

Painting of Zoroaster

Other religions today have similar ideas. The angels described in Christian teachings along with the notion of a hell waiting for evildoers originated in the teachings of Zoroaster. Zoroastrianism is still practiced by about 140,000 followers today, with the largest groups being in India and Iran.

CHAPTER X:

THE PEOPLE TODAY

The people in present-day Iran are faced with the same challenges of ancient times. Mountains, deserts, and scarcity of water influence today's culture just as they did in ancient times, especially in undeveloped **rural** areas. In 1935, the country's name was changed from Persia to Iran, which is much smaller than the Persia of ancient times. Iran's capital, Tehran, is the largest city and the political, commercial, and industrial center of the nation. Iran's current population is more than 70 million people with nearly 12 million people living in the Tehran area.

Petroleum is the rich mineral resource of Iran today. About 64% of the world's oil lies under the shallow saltwater lake known as the Persian Gulf. Additionally, Iran is located next to Asia, which has the world's second largest undeveloped natural gas reserves. Any pipelines that would carry oil for export must cross Iran. With so much of the world dependent upon oil and gas, Iran holds a very important position in political and social decisions around the globe.

In addition to its petroleum products, Iran's chief exports are carpets, fruits, nuts, animal hides, iron, and steel. Machinery, metals, military supplies, food, and chemicals are brought into the country from trading partners such as Japan, Germany, and Italy.

The Shah-en-shah Monument in Tehran

The capital city of Tehran was formerly the capital of the Persian Empire. More than half the country's industry is based in Tehran. Electrical equipment, textiles, sugar, and cement are manufactured, and motor vehicles are assembled there. The city's large open market is the leading center for the sale and export of carpets.

Remnants of a complex pattern of ethnic groups, languages, and regions remain today with more than 400 different tribes in modern Iran. This diversity causes many of the conflicts that arise today, as well as those that have been handed down throughout Iran's history. While there has been a blending of most tribes, some still live in remote mountain and desert areas. In their isolation, they have been able to keep their ancient customs, languages, and religions alive.

Modern Iranians getting ready to take a bus to Syria

A TIMELINE OF THE
HISTORY OF PERSIA

2000-1800 B.C.E.   Aryan migration from Southern Russia to Near East

628 B.C.E.   Birth of Zoroaster, the Persian Prophet

559-529 B.C.E.   Reign of Cyrus the Great

547 B.C.E   Cyrus defeats King Croesus of Lydia

529-522 B.C.E   Reign of Cambyses II
Cambyses II conquers Egypt

521-486 B.C.E   Reign of Darius I

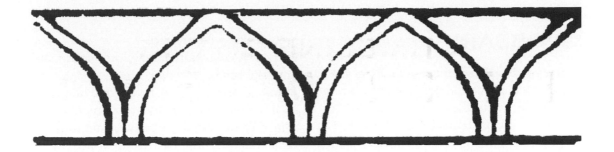

513-512 B.C.E.	First Asian Invasion of Europe, Persians conquer Thrace and Macedon
490 B.C.E.	Persians defeated by Greeks, Battle of Marathon
486-465 B.C.E.	Reign of Xerxes I, son of Darius I
480 B.C.E.	Persians defeated by Greeks at Salamis
330 B.C.E.	Alexander the Great destroys Persian Empire, Persepolis Burned

GLOSSARY

Achaemenids: The ruling house of ancient Persia, generally considered important from the reign of Cyrus the Great (559 B.C.E.) to the overthrow of Darius III in 330 B.C.E. The word comes from the Greek form, Achaimenes.

Ahura Mazda: The Wise Lord, a god of the Zoroastrianism religion in Persia. He is worshiped by the Zoroastrians as the good god.

Alexander the Great: Young warrior king of Macedonia.

Armenia: A former kingdom of western Asia in the mountainous region southeast of the Black Sea and southwest of the Caspian Sea. The area is now divided among Armenia, Turkey, and Iran.

Bactria: Ancient Greek name of the country between the range of Hindu Kush (Paropamisus) and the Amu Darya (Oxus) with the capital Bactra (now Balkh). It was known to the east in the Indian subcontinent as Gandhara.

B.C.E.: "Before the Common Era," or before the year "1." This term is similar to using B.C., which refers to time before the birth of Christ. B.C.E. is a non-religious phrase for the same time period.

Carmania: Ancient region, also known as Kerman, in southeast Iran bordering on the Gulf of Oman and Persian Gulf south of ancient Parthia.

Conduit: A passage through which water can pass.

Cuneiform: A system of writing using "wedge-shaped" characters created by the ancient Sumerians.

Daric: A gold coin of ancient Persia with the figure of an archer on one side.

Domesticated: An animal or plant that has been brought in close contact with and used to the advantage of humans.

Dynasty: A succession of rulers of the same family line that maintains its position for a considerable length of time.

Elam: Ancient mighty kingdom in what is present-day, western Iraq.

Empire: A collection of kingdoms under one powerful ruler.

Ethnic: Distinctive of the ways of living, such as shared nationality, tribal membership, religion, language, cultural and traditional customs built by a group of people.

Fertile Crescent: A region of western Asia that is shaped like a quarter moon and covers present-day Iraq, Syria, Lebanon, and Israel.

Gandhara: An ancient region in northwest India and eastern Afghanistan.

Ionia: An ancient region in western Asia Minor bordering on the Aegean Sea west of Lydia.

Iran: Country in southwest Asia that is bordered on the north by the Caspian Sea and on the south by the Persian Gulf and Gulf of Oman.

Kushites: An Afro-Asiatic mountain people of Mesopotamia from whom came Nimrod, who was king of Assyria.

Lydia: In ancient times the name of an area of western Anatolia (Turkey) that was fertile and rich in minerals.

Macedonia: An ancient kingdom in northern Greece, centralized under Phillip II, who, with his son, Alexander the Great, created a vast empire in the 4th century B.C.E.

Medes: Natives of ancient Media in Persia, located in an area from the Caspian Sea to the Zagros Mountains.

Mesopotamia: An area located between the Tigris and Euphrates rivers, which was the site of the world's first civilization. The Greek word means "land between two rivers."

Murghab: A river rising in northeast Afghanistan and flowing about 530 miles (853 km) generally west and northwest to the Kara Kim Desert in southeast Turkmenistan.

Nineveh: An ancient Assyrian city on the Tigris across from the modern city of Mosul in the northern part of what is now Iraq.

Nomad: Person having no fixed place to live

and who moves from place to place within a specific area when the season changes or they are in search of food.

Old Persian: The official language of the ancient Persian empire during the time of the Achaemenid kings.

Paradesios: A Persian word meaning enclosure, from which our word "paradise" came. The walls enclosed beautiful green gardens for the king's pleasure.

Pars: An ancient province of Persia that formed the center of the Persian Empire. The capital of Persepolis was located there.

Persia: An empire in southern Asia created by Cyrus the Great in the 6th century B.C.E. and destroyed by Alexander the Great in the 4th century B.C.E.

Persis: Greek word for the people who moved to the "land of Aryan" and built the vast empire known as Persia.

Phoenicians: People of an ancient country in southwest Asia at the east end of the Mediterranean Sea in modern Lebanon.

Portico: A porch or entrance to a building consisting of a covered and often columned area.

Rural: Country people or life.

Sardis: An ancient Greek city located in the western part of what is now modern Turkey. As the capital of Lydia, Sardis was the cultural center of Asia Minor.

Sash: A band of material around the waist of a skirt or trousers.

Satrap: A governor of a province in ancient Persia.

Scythians: A nomadic people who lived in Scythia, an ancient area of Eurasia extending from the Black Sea to the Aral Sea from the 8th to the 4th century B.C.E.

Steppe: A plain without trees and apart from rivers or lakes. From the Russian word "steppe," the plain may be semi-desert or covered with grass or shrubs, or both, depending on the season.

Tribute: Payment by one nation for protection by another.

Zoroastrianism: A system of religion founded in Persia in the 6th century B.C.E. by Zoroaster and based on the struggle between light (good) and dark (evil).

Books of Interest

Cotterell, Arthur. *The Encyclopedia of Ancient Civilizations*. Penguin Books, 1980.

Mackay, Sandra. *The Iranians: Persia, Islam and the Soul of a Nation*. Plume, 1998.

Roberts, J. M. *The New History of the World*. Oxford Press, 2002.

Web Sites

http://www.zoroastriankids.com/539bc.html

http://www.geocities.com/ladysveva/clothing/Persian.html

http://www.historyforkids.org/learn/westasia/history/persians.htm

INDEX

Katherine E. Reece is a native of Georgia, where she grew up in a small town located in the foothills of the Blue Ridge Mountains. She has traveled throughout the United States, Europe, Australia, and New Zealand. Katherine completed her Bachelor of Fine Arts with an emphasis in studio art at the University of Colorado in Boulder, Colorado, where she now resides. Her extensive studies in art history gives her an appreciation for all that can be learned about the culture, beliefs, and traditions of ancient civilizations from the architecture, artifacts, and recordings that have been preserved through the centuries.